Our World of Information

Put it together

Using Information

Claire Throp

Heinemann
LIBRARY

www.heinemannlibrary.co.uk
Visit our website to find out more information about Heinemann Library books.

To order:

☎ Phone +44 (0) 1865 888066

▤ Fax +44 (0) 1865 314091

💻 Visit www.heinemannlibrary.co.uk

Heinemann Library is an imprint of Capstone Global Library Limited, a company incorporated in England and Wales having its registered office at 7 Pilgrim Street, London, EC4V 6LB - Registered company number: 6695582

"Heinemann" is a registered trademark of Pearson Education Limited, under licence to Capstone Global Library Limited

Text © Capstone Global Library Limited 2010
First published in hardback in 2010

Edited by Charlotte Guillain and Catherine Veitch
Designed by Richard Parker
Original illustrations © Capstone Global Library
Illustrated by Darren Lingard
Picture research by Ruth Blair
Originated by Heinemann Library
Printed in China by South China Printing Company Ltd.

ISBN 978 0 431163 14 7 (hardback)
14 13 12 11 10
10 9 8 7 6 5 4 3 2 1

British Library Cataloguing in Publication Data
Throp, Claire.
Put it together : using information. -- (Our world of information)
001-dc22
A full catalogue record for this book is available from the British Library.

Acknowledgements

We would like to thank the following for permission to reproduce photographs: Alamy pp. **8** (© Tetra Images), **11** (© Ian Shaw), **17** (© Blackout Concepts), **21** (© Pablo Paul), **24** (© Vikki Martin); © Capstone Publishers pp. **10** & **14** (Karon Dubke); Corbis pp. **5** (Tom Stewart), **6** (LWA-JDC), **13**, **15** (LWA-Dann Tardif/Zefa), **28** (Jutta Klee); Getty Images pp. **18** (Tim Platt), **22** (Elyse Lewin), **25**; iStockphoto p. **26**; Photoshot p. **23** (Blend Images); Shutterstock p. **27** (© Dmitriy Shironosov).

Cover photograph of a child using a computer for school work reproduced with permission of Corbis (Jose Luis Pelaez, Inc.).

Every effort has been made to contact copyright holders of material reproduced in this book. Any omissions will be rectified in subsequent printings if notice is given to the publishers.

Contents

Any words appearing in the text in bold, **like this**, are explained in the glossary.

What is information?

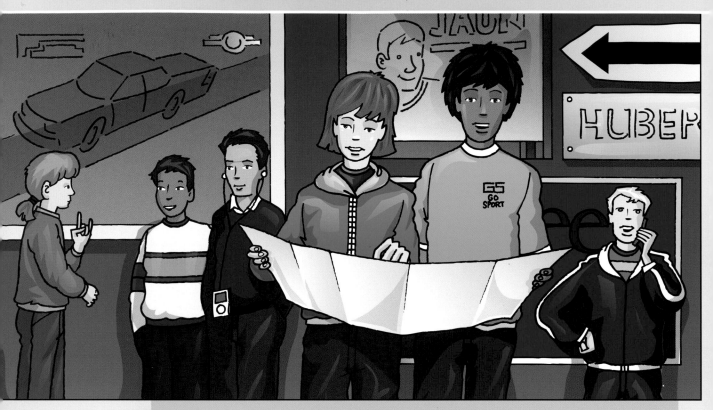

 Information is all around us, on signs, posters, the radio and mobile phones. Where else can you find information?

You are surrounded by information. Information is what people know about things. It can be **sign language**, photographs, text, or many other things. Information can be used for talks and presentations, **projects**, and for finding out about clubs.

4

Leabharlanna Poibli Chathair Bhaile Átha Cliath
Dublin City Public Libraries

People often need to use information in different ways. You might need to use information for a school project, for example. Or you might want to share the information that you have found with friends, family, and classmates.

 You can find lots of information in books.

Where might you need to use information?

There are many times that you will need to use information. You might use information for schoolwork or a hobby.

 School is a great place for finding out and using information.

If you travel to a new place, you might look at **maps** before you go. When you are nearly there, you might ask someone for final **directions**. The map and the directions will help you get where you want to go.

Listening

 Writing information down can help you to remember it.

When you are hearing information, good listening skills are important. If you do not **concentrate** when someone is telling you something, you may forget what they have said or not use the information correctly.

Sometimes you have to use the information you are given straightaway. If you ask someone how to do something, you need to listen very carefully. You may even need to write some notes so that you can use the information correctly.

 Sometimes you will need to ask more questions after you get an answer.

Answer the question

What was school like when your grandparents were young?

Always check that you have written down the question correctly.

For schoolwork, you need to make sure that you find the right information for whatever question or **project** you are working on. You can use a system to help you organize information. One idea is to break down the question or project into several parts.

 Breaking down the question helps you understand what it means.

Think about what you want to say or write for each part and look at the information that you have. For example, the main question might be "Find out what school was like when your grandparents were children." You could break it down into different parts – the classroom, schoolbooks, and outdoor activities.

No copying!

 Will you learn anything from copying your friend's work?

When something has been **published**, the information in it belongs to the writer or to the publisher. If someone else copies from the text using exactly the same words, it is the same as stealing someone else's belongings.

You can use books, the Internet, and other **sources** of information to get general ideas or facts. If you need to use the exact words you find in a text, be careful to say where that text comes from and who wrote it.

 When you use information, you must make sure that you do not steal other people's work.

Understanding information

One of the best ways to avoid copying other people's work is to use a range of **sources**. You could find out about the same thing from a book, a website, television, and a newspaper or magazine. That way you also get to **cross-check** facts and make sure they are correct.

 If you find it difficult to rewrite information in your own words, it may be that you do not fully understand it.

If you do not understand some information, ask an adult for help. Your teacher or a librarian will be able to talk things through with you, so you have a clear understanding of the information in your mind.

An adult will help you find a source of information that makes sense to you.

Pictures

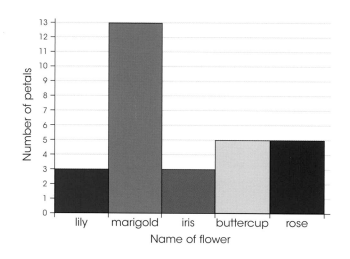

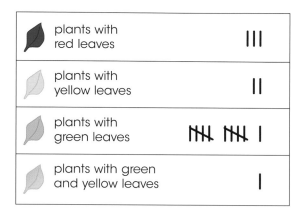

	plants with red leaves	III
	plants with yellow leaves	II
	plants with green leaves	ЖЖ I
	plants with green and yellow leaves	I

 Bar charts and tables can be colourful and help to break up text.

Using pictures can make your work more useful and interesting. You can include charts, tables, and other **graphic organizers**. Photos and drawings can also be full of information. Try taking photos yourself or ask an adult to help you.

For example, you might have been given a school **project** on the life cycle of sunflowers. You could take photos of a seed, a small plant beginning to grow, the sunflower fully grown, and finally the sunflower dying.

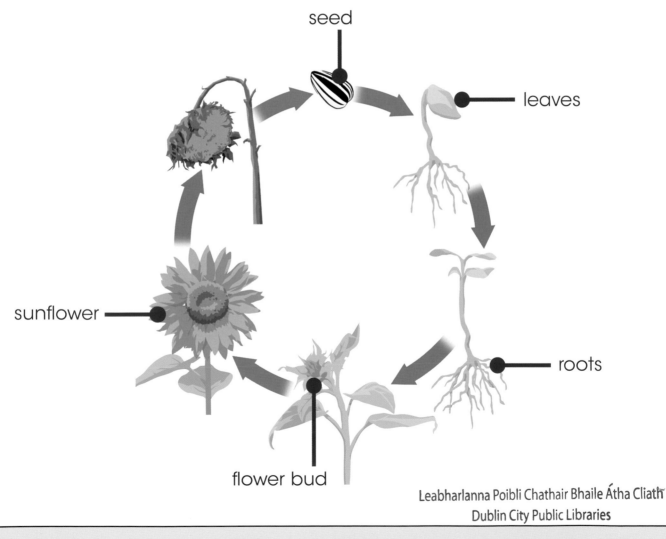

seed

leaves

roots

flower bud

sunflower

Spoken information

Sometimes you need to use an object to present information to your class. For example, a photo of your grandparent's class would help you explain to your friends what school was like when your grandparent was a child.

 You can share information in a group discussion.

Your teacher shares information with you and the rest of your class every day. The main way that your teacher does this is by talking to you and telling you what he or she knows.

 You too can share information by talking to your class.

Online information

If there are several people working on a **project**, you can use the Internet to share information. You could do this using **instant messaging**. You could also use a **wiki**. This is a website that allows several people to add or change information.

 You can send your part of a project to friends as an **email** attachment.

You should only open attachments or share information when you know who or where it is from. Attachments from friends and family are usually safe.

 Be careful when opening email attachments.

Choices

You can use information to help you make choices. If you are trying to decide whether to join a new club you could look up their website. You could also ask friends who are in the club what they think.

Friends can be a good source of information.

Decisions such as where to go on holiday can be difficult. Your parents may get leaflets about holidays from a travel agent. You could also pay a visit to the library and use their **online catalogue** to find information **sources**, such as books about different countries.

 After reading all the information, you and your family can decide where you would like to visit.

Other ways of using information

Sometimes information is put together in special ways. Visually impaired people read a **language** called Braille. Braille is a system of raised dots that stand for letters and numbers.

 People who are deaf may use **sign language**, a system of hand movements that stand for spoken words.

Sometimes meetings take place where people speak different languages. Someone who can speak several languages is called an **interpreter**. He or she **translates** what is being said, so that everyone can understand what is going on.

 Ear pieces allow people to hear the interpreter.

Sharing information

 You can find information quickly if you share the work with friends.

Information can be used in many ways. You might need to use it for group **projects** at school. You might use information to help you make decisions.

Communicating with other people is an important way of using information. Sharing information that you have found helps everybody to learn new things.

 Information can be used to tell others how you feel about something.

Activities

Best friend poster

Make a poster about your best friend. You could put their name at the top and then include some photos of them. Write captions for each photo to explain what is happening in the picture or how old your friend was at the time. You might want to put the pictures in time order. This is called a **timeline**.

Rewriting practice

Copying other people's work is wrong. It is a good idea to practise putting information into your own words. Read the following two pieces of text, for a leaflet telling children how to recycle, and then try to rewrite the information in your own words.

People use different materials, such as paper, glass, metal, and plastic, every day. These materials are very useful, but sometimes they are wasted. When you throw materials away you make waste. Recycling is when people change waste items into things that can be used again. You should recycle as much as possible to help look after the planet. Take glass to a glass bank and use a recycling box for paper and tins. Most cities and towns have recycling collections that have been set up by the council.

Things that can be recycled:

- paper
- card
- foil
- tins
- glass bottles
- plastic bottles
- newspapers and magazines.

Glossary

communicate sharing information or ideas

concentrate think about one particular thing at a time

cross-check checking a particular piece of information in a number of sources

directions explanation for how to get to a certain place or how to do something

email electronic mail. These are messages that are sent from one computer to another.

graphic organizer way of showing information in a chart, table, or graph

instant messaging way of talking to other people through connected computers. It is different from email because it happens as though you were talking face-to-face.

interpreter person who can speak different languages, and tells other people what is being said so that they can understand

language set of words that people use to share information. People in different countries use different words but they mean the same thing.

map picture of a particular area, such as your town, to show where things are. A map often includes roads, streets, parks, and important buildings.

online catalogue electronic list of all the information sources, such as books, films, and magazines, that can be found in a particular library. The list can be accessed by computer.

project task set by a teacher that can be done on your own or with other people

published printed materials, such as books and magazines, produced for sale

sign language system of hand movements to stand for spoken words

source place in which we can find things such as information. Books, television, and websites on the Internet are sources of information.

timeline arrangement of pictures or text in the order they happened in time

translate to change from one language to another

wiki website that allows many people to add or change information

Find out more

Books

A Trip to the Library, Kate Hayden (Dorling Kindersley, 2004)

My First Internet Guide, Chris Oxlade (Heinemann Library, 2007)

Websites

Yahoo! Kids – Homework Help
http://kids.yahoo.com/learn
This website includes links to an encyclopedia, dictionary, maps, and lots of other useful websites.

Ask Kids – Schoolhouse
www.askkids.com/schoolhouse?pch=sch
Ask Kids is a great search engine specially created for use by children.

BBC – Students
www.bbc.co.uk/schools/students/
This website includes lots of activities and games to help you learn.

Index